To:

_____

From:

_____

May the LORD give you the desire of your heart
and make all your plans succeed.

Psalm 20:4

now what?

God's Guide to Life
for Graduates

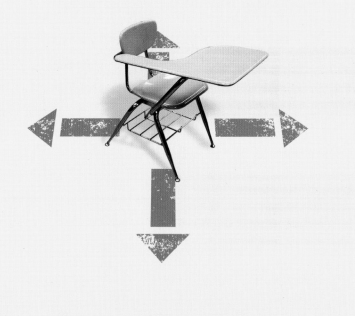

John Ortberg

Contents

Congratulations!
This Is Your Moment.

I believe the greatest moment of your life is this moment right now. It's this tick of the clock, because this moment is where God is.

The God who made the psalmist say,
"This is the day that the LORD has made;
let us rejoice and be glad in it"
has made this moment just for you. It is this day,
this moment, not the one that's gone, not the one
that's coming.

People can lose their whole lives by being scared about some moment in the future. People waste years being nostalgic about some moment that's gone in the past. Don't spend your moment wishing you could occupy somebody else's moment—because it doesn't belong to you, and it never will.

I believe you ought to expect this moment to be the greatest moment of your life. Not because it's easy. Not because you're so strong or so clever. Not because it's going to be a Kodak moment (although your parents, grandparents and friends will try real hard to make it one), but because somewhere about 10,000 miles away from here, on the outskirts of Jerusalem, there is an empty tomb. And if Jesus is not laying in that tomb, then where is he? He's right here, right now, because this moment is where Jesus is. And right now is your little slice of eternity when it is fueled with God.

+

Do it with
Passion.

God gives everybody work to do, whether you get paid for it or not, whether you're a volunteer, whether you do work in an office, at a church, whether you go to school, whether you do it at home, in the neighborhood or in an office. God made us to contribute, to create, to produce value and make the world a better place.

Therefore, my beloved brethren, be steadfast, immovable, always abounding in the work of the Lord, knowing that your labor is not in vain in the Lord.

1 Corinthians 15:58 (NKJV)

Work itself is part of what God does. God creates, and he made us in his image to do work, to create. That's a real good thing. And God says over and over again in Scripture, "I want you to excel at what you do. I want you to abound. I want you to take the gifts and talents that I've given you and develop into the fullest potential you're capable of. I want you to discover the deepest passions that are hardwired into you, and I want you to fan them into flames. I want you to make a difference in this world."

Whatever your hand finds to do,
do it with all your might.
Ecclesiastes 9:10

The very best thing we can hope for is, when we get to the end of our lives, to be able to say to God, "I abounded in the work you gave me to do. It may or may not have looked very impressive to other people. It wasn't perfect by a long shot. But whatever my hand found for me to do, I really did try to do with all my might. I tried to work with all my heart, as though I was doing it for you, God."

He sought his God and worked wholeheartedly. And so he prospered.

2 Chronicles 31:21

**When man
loses the sacred
significance of work
and of himself as
worker, he soon loses
the sacred meaning
of time and of life.**

Carl F. H. Henry

Be strong and do the work.

1 Chronicles 28:10

Trust in the LORD with all your heart
and lean not on your own understanding;
in all your ways acknowledge him,
and he will make your paths straight.

Proverbs 3:5-6

We don't work primarily for money. We work for the experience of being highly motivated to do things, of being positive and hopeful. We work for that sense of accomplishment in doing good things. We work for the experience of having an ongoing flow of creative ideas and energy to make them happen, to see them realized.

Work is an extension of personality. It is achievement. It is one of the ways in which a person defines himself, measures his worth, and his humanity.

Peter F. Drucker

Work is *Essential*

In the beginning God
created the heavens and the earth.

Genesis 1:1

Ever wonder what God does all day? Does he just sit around and watch stuff? Is he involved in hobbies? Do they have sack races with the Trinity or something like that? What does God actually do?

Well, in a single word, God works.

The opening lines of the Bible are filled with verbs that describe God's action. He *separated* light from darkness. He *made* the sky and the solid ground. He *gathered* the water together into the seas. He *created* plants and living creatures. He *formed* human beings. God worked at the very beginning. But then after the sixth day, he didn't go into retirement. Psalm 104 says that the universe doesn't run by mechanical necessity. It's run by God.

God makes springs pour water into the ravines;
  it flows between the mountains. . . .
He waters the mountains from his upper chambers;
  the earth is satisfied by the fruit of his work.
He makes grass grow for the cattle,
  and plants for man to cultivate—
  bringing forth food from the earth. . . .

How many are your works, O LORD!
  In wisdom you made them all;
  the earth is full of your creatures. . . .
These all look to you
  to give them their food at the proper time.
When you give it to them,
  they gather it up;
when you open your hand,
  they are satisfied with good things.

Psalm 104:10, 13–14, 24, 27–28

God is running his universe every day, but the Bible makes it clear he is particularly busy working with people—people like you and me. The psalmist wrote in Psalm 121, "The God who watches over Israel will neither slumber nor sleep" (verse 4). But he's always busy guarding and guiding and protecting and watching over his people.

At the climax of God's work in the creation story, the Bible says, "The LORD God formed the man from the dust of the ground and breathed into his nostrils the breath of life, and the man became a living being" (Genesis 2:7). Now because you were made in his image, a piece of work by God, you were also created to do work. You were created for work, among other things. People get confused about this sometimes. Often people think that work is a result of the Fall— that before Adam and Eve sinned, nobody had any work to do. But according to the Bible, God is a worker. And before Adam and Eve sinned, the Bible says, "The LORD God took the man and put him in the Garden of Eden to work it and take care of it" (Genesis 2:15).

God created human beings in his image to work, to create value, to produce, to labor; and that was all *before* the Fall. So work is essential to your humanity.

There are different kinds of gifts,
but the same Spirit distributes them.
There are different kinds of service,
but the same Lord.
There are different kinds of working,
but in all of them and
in everyone it is the same God at work.

1 Corinthians 12:4-6 (TNIV)

When God wanted
sponges and oysters, he
made them, and he put
one on a rock and the
other in the mud. When
he made man, he did not
make him to be a sponge
or an oyster; he made him
with feet and hands, and
head and heart, and vital
blood, and a place to use
them, and he said to him,
"Go work."

Henry Ward Beecher

The God of the Bible is preeminently a worker. He is highly interested in work. He understands the joys and the fulfillment of work, and he's deeply committed to it.

Work matters because God notices what you do. You might want to put a little sign on your desk that says, "I am working for God," because you really are.

So every skilled person to whom the LORD has given skill and ability to know how to carry out all the work . . . are to do the work just as the LORD has commanded.

Exodus 36:1

Your Calling is Calling:
Go Find it

Every human being on this earth has a calling. There are no un-called human beings. You have a purpose. You have a design. It was conceived by God, and it is essential to God's dream for the human community.

A calling is not primarily about increasing your earning potential or status or prestige. A calling refers to the fact that God made you with certain capacities, and this world *needs* you to use those abilities.

To fulfill your calling is a noble thing. It's at the core of human existence. If you watch people who are fulfilling their callings, their motivation level is high; when obstacles come along, they have amazing endurance to overcome them. They're growing and learning, and there's joy in what they do. To miss out on your calling is to miss out on a large part of the reason why you walk this planet, and why you were made by God.

Some people think that only certain categories of folks have a calling—pastors, maybe, or Billy Graham, or Mother Teresa. That's not true. The Bible is very, very clear that whether your job is in a church or in the world of business, wherever it is, every human being is created by God, gifted by God, and called by God. You have a calling, and you had better take your calling seriously.

It's very important for you to find what God had in mind when he first thought you up. A calling is something you *discover*, not something you *choose*, so I want to give you some questions to help you find your calling:

1. What's My Raw Material?
God has given you DNA, certain predispositions, a temperament, and talents, and you have to honor this

raw material that you've been given. So you need to ask yourself questions like, "What sorts of things do other people tell me I do well?" or, "What have I done well in the past?" Write down your important life achievements. What were some things in the early days of your life that you were good at?

2. What Work Brings Me Joy?

What do you have a desire for—a passion? It's not an accident that your spirit rejoices in certain activities. That, too, is part of what God has placed in you. What do you love to do? What is it that brings you to life?

3. What Are My Expectations?

There's a big difference between loving to do certain activities or tasks for their own sake because you were made to love them, and wanting a job because you think you want the rewards or status or prestige that might flow out of it. There's a big difference between doing a task because God calls you to it, and just doing what your father, or friends, or your ego wants you to do.

4. What Are My Limitations?

What's the one limitation in your life that is the most painful for you to accept? If you can acknowledge and embrace all of your limitedness, you will have made tremendous strides down the road to understanding your calling.

According to the Bible, you have a calling, and it has to do with what God hardwired into you. You must seek it with an open, submitted spirit. When people try to pretend that they're something they're not, they live with a chronic sense of inadequacy. They set themselves up for a lifetime of frustrations. Don't do that. Be ruthlessly open to the truth about yourself. Your calling is something you discover, not something you choose.

> **The place God calls you to is the place where your deep gladness and the world's deep hunger meet.**
>
> Frederick Buechner

> The one who plants and the one who waters have one purpose, and they will each be rewarded according to their own labor. For we are God's co-workers; you are God's field, God's building.
>
> 1 Corinthians 3:8–9 (TNIV)

Whatever you do, work at it with all your heart,
as working for the Lord, not for human masters.

Colossians 3:23 (TNIV)

All to whom God gives wealth and possessions
and whom he enables to enjoy them, and to
accept their lot and find enjoyment in their toil—
this is the gift of God.

Ecclesiastes 5:19 (NRSV)

Doing what God requires is a sign of superior wisdom. God requires that you work hard at your calling without worrying about what anyone else is doing.

Martin Luther

It seems as if God gives
us hints each day about
what he'd like us to do.
If you look closely
around you, or if you
listen carefully to what
a friend says, I bet you
will recognize a
potential hint as
to what God would
like you to do.
Listen carefully.
Observe.
God is pointing
the direction.

Christopher de Vinck

Money Isn't
Everything

A lot of people in our world think the goal of work is to accumulate enough money so that you can quit working! But the idea that your life's work is all about accumulating enough stuff is fundamentally at odds with what Scripture says. Of course, a part of work is to be able to meet the basic needs of yourself and your family—that's an important thing, but if your work is not meaningful to you, if it's not connected to God's call on your life, eventually you'll resent it. It doesn't make any difference how much money you make. Money alone is not worth giving that much of your life to.

If the main thing you're working for is a paycheck, you're going to resent it. A mere paycheck is not worth giving your life to. Money is not the primary reason that God calls us to work.

Whoever loves money never has money enough;
whoever loves wealth is never satisfied
with his income.

Ecclesiastes 5:10

The love of money is a root of all kinds of evil.

1 Timothy 6:10

Jesus said, "No one can serve two masters.
Either he will hate the one and love the other,
or he will be devoted to the one and despise the
other. You cannot serve both God and Money."

Matthew 6:24

Someone who's
obsessed with making
money to the exclusion
of other goals in life
has likely forgone the
possibility of the
acceptance in
God's kingdom.

Jimmy Carter

A man's treatment
of money is the most
decisive test of his
character—how he
makes it and
how he spends it.

James Moffatt

If a person gets
his attitude toward
money straight,
it will help straighten
out almost every
other area in his life.

Billy Graham

Don't Throw Your Life
Away Over Money

It costs something when Jesus calls you.

I have a friend. He's a businessman. He's in his seventies now. But years ago, I attended his church one time on a Sunday when he gave a terrific message. We talked afterwards, and he said to me, "You know, when I was a young man, I always felt that I ought to go into pastoral ministry."

And I asked him, "Why didn't you?"

Well, when it came right down to it, it was just money. He was already into the business world, and he was doing quite well. So he didn't follow what he sensed was God's calling on his life.

Friends, I don't know how else to say this. *It's only money.* But people get all twisted up in knots over it, and they stay awake at night thinking about it, and they stew and they worry and they get anxious and they scheme and they trade away their integrity, only to get a little pile, a little more of it. And their hearts get all knotted up, and they worry that somebody else might get ahold of it. And they throw away their lives running after more of it.

But *it's only money.* It's never a reason not to follow Christ. It's never a reason not to do the thing that God needs you to do. It's only money.

When you work—whether you love it or whether it's not real thrilling to you—you ought to give it the best that you have when you're there. But don't give it time or energy or allegiance that keeps you from living in the way of Christ. It's not worth it.

Keep your lives
free from the love of money
and be content
with what you have.

Hebrews 13:5

You may say to yourself,
"My power and the strength of my hands
have produced this wealth for me."
But remember the LORD your God, for it is he
who gives you the ability to produce wealth,
and so confirms his covenant.

Deuteronomy 8:17-18

Work in
Jesus' name

We all work. We all create value—that's what work is: the creation of value to enhance this creation that God has given us.

What would it look like for you to work in Jesus' name? Well, first, work becomes something that you do together with him. You were not meant to work on your own. So, tomorrow, take a moment at the beginning of your workday when you sit down at your desk, or before a computer, or in your home, and invite Jesus to partner with you. Tell him, "Today, just for this day, I'm not going to work by myself."

Any time through your workday when you have a tough problem, ask him for help. When you have a difficult decision to make, ask him for wisdom, and then listen and really be open. When you find your energy flagging, ask him for renewed strength.

When you find your attitude going south, ask him to re-orient your heart.

Put a symbol on your desk or wall where you can see it to remind you that today you and Jesus are partnering together in your work. Maybe it's just one word: peace, or wisdom, or joy, or diligence. Every few hours as you're working, pause for two or three minutes. Close the door (if you have one), look out the window (if you have one), and just remember that God is at work in the whole world. Thank him for his help. Rest with him for a moment, hand him your worries, and ask for his energy.

Work is the means of living, but it is not living.
Josiah Gilbert Holland

Every moment of every day is an opportunity to be with Jesus. When you forget—and you will, when you mess up—and you will, remember this really important rule: There's to be no beating yourself up! Every moment is another chance. God just keeps sending them. That's grace. Every moment is a new chance for you to be with him.

We work to become, not to acquire.
Elbert Hubbard

In the business world, everyone is paid in two coins: cash and experience. Take the experience first; the cash will come later.
Harold Geneen

**If you lose yourself in
your work, you find
who you are.**

Frederick Buechner

Everyone should be quick to listen,
slow to speak and slow to become angry,
for man's anger does not bring
about the righteous life that God desires.

James 1:19-20

How to Keep
Your Job
(Once you get one)

A researcher, William Menninger, found that when people lose their job, up to 80 percent of the time, they don't lose it because of technical incompetence. It's not because they don't know how to do the technical aspects of their job. They lose their job because of relational incompetence, because they don't know how to relate effectively to people. If you master the three instructions that James gives in the New Testament, the likelihood of that happening in your life will go down to just about zero.

These three pointers from James are so elemental that anybody can do them. You don't need lots of training or an advanced degree. You can do them. You can start today. They're essential, they're simple, they're memorable, they're elemental. It's about as simple as it can be—one quick and two slows.

1. Be Quick to Listen.

People who stay calm have real insight. After all, even a fool may be thought wise and intelligent if he just stays quiet and keeps his mouth shut. Even if you do nothing else, if you learn to be slow to speak, at least you'll avoid saying stupid things. People will think you're wise. You'll get a reputation for wisdom, for being a sage, if you just stay quiet.

2. Be Slow to Speak.

What's at the heart of this concern is, don't talk too much, don't talk without thinking, don't speak foolishly, don't speak rashly, and don't run off at the mouth! Just assess yourself. If you talk too much or too fast, here are three tips to slow you down:

• Stop: Just stop talking. Inhale. Let there be silence for a moment.

• Practice not interrupting. When the other person is speaking, don't speak. Allow the other person to

continue what it is they're saying until
they're through.

> A fool gives full vent to his anger,
> but a wise man keeps himself
> under control.
>
> Proverbs 29:11

• Ask yourself: Why am I talking too much?
Maybe it's because of fear. Maybe it's because of
insecurity. Maybe it's because of anxiety or the
need to control. Maybe you feel the need to
impress other people, to let them know how smart
you are, or what you've read, or what you think.
But I think that the reason most human beings talk
too much is that they have a hard time trusting
that God really will be effective in the situation, so
instead they need to control, or impress, or domi-
nate, or whatever. Stop it. Trust God instead.

3. Be Slow to Anger.

If you observe the first two principles, you will tend
to come out all right on number three. If you carefully

cultivate the habit of listening well, and if you cultivate the habit of speaking thoughtfully and with restraint, if you're quick to listen and slow to speak, then you will automatically be slow to anger. It'll just happen.

You can make progress on these three, and you can start today. If you will do it consistently year after year, you will get to the end of your life and will say to yourself, *I'm so grateful that I took the wisdom of God seriously.*

Work is the natural exercise and function of man.... Work is not primarily a thing one does to live, but the thing one lives to do. It is, or should be, the full expression of the worker's faculties, the thing in which he finds spiritual, mental, and bodily satisfaction, and the medium in which he offers himself to God.

Dorothy L. Sayers

Fare $2.00

Whatever you do, whether in word or deed,
do it all in the name of the Lord Jesus,
giving thanks to God the Father through him.

Colossians 3:17

Make *how* you work an expression of *who* you are.
Put yourself into it—whether you're studying,
or doing things at home, or working on the job.

Do your work in such a way that if somebody were to
look at what you have just worked on, you would be
comfortable in saying, "This is a reflection of who
I am, of what my standards are, of what God made
me to do."

Put yourself into it. Do it with your whole heart,
whatever the task is. The key thing is not the task.
The key thing is whether or not you're doing it in a
wholehearted way. When people do this, it makes
a huge difference in the quality of their work and of
their hearts.

May the God of peace, who through the blood
of the eternal covenant brought back
from the dead our Lord Jesus, that great Shepherd
of the sheep, equip you with everything good
for doing his will, and may he work in us what is
pleasing to him, through Jesus Christ,
to whom be glory for ever and ever. Amen.

Hebrews 13:20–21

*God's dwelling place is now among the people,
and he will dwell with them.
They will be his people, and God himself
will be with them and be their God.*

Revelation 21:3 (TNIV)

God's constant desire is that you should be, in every aspect, a dwelling place for him. You—your life—should be, in every aspect, a dwelling place for God. Jesus said right before he left the earth, "Don't be afraid. For surely I am with you always, even to the ends of the earth." He sends his Spirit so that your life can be the temple of the Holy Spirit. You can be the house of God.

Eliminate

Hurry

*Desire without knowledge is not good,
and one who moves too hurriedly misses
the way.*

Proverbs 19:2 (NRSV)

When I first moved to Chicago, to Willow Creek Church, I called a friend of mine—the wisest spiritual man that I know—and I asked him, "What do I need to do to be healthy spiritually? What do I need to do to guard my heart?"

There was a long pause.

Then he said, "You must ruthlessly eliminate hurry from your life."

There was another long pause, and I finally said, "Okay, I wrote that one down. Now, what else do you have to tell me, because I don't have much time, and I want to get a lot of wisdom out of this conversation."

He replied, "There is nothing else. Hurry is the great enemy of spiritual life in our day. It has had other enemies in other days. In our day, in our world, hurry is the great enemy of spiritual life, because you can hardly do anything the way that Jesus did it if you are in a hurry. You cannot love in a hurry. You cannot listen to a child in a hurry.

"Jesus was often busy. But there's a real important distinction between hurry and busy. Busy is an external condition—a condition of the body. Jesus was often busy, but he was never hurried. Hurried is a condition of the soul. It is an inward condition in which you are so frantic and preoccupied that you are unable to receive love from the Father, and unable to be present with other people, to give love to them."

Things will not settle down in life. And if you wait to get around to what really matters, you will never do what God made you to do or be. Your soul will wither and die. Hurry is the great enemy of spiritual life in our day, and you must ruthlessly eliminate hurry from your life. No one else will do this for you—not your boss, or your spouse, or your kids, or your parents. You must do this for yourself.

The fear of the LORD leads to life:
Then one rests content, untouched by trouble.

Proverbs 19:23

You will not leave in haste
    or go in flight;
    for the LORD will go before you,
the God of Israel will be your rear guard.

Isaiah 52:12

Dead things cannot
grow. Before there
can be spiritual
growth, there must
be spiritual life.

George Sweeting

God has a program
of character
development for each
one of us. He wants
others to look at
our lives and say,
"He walks with God,
for he lives
like Christ."

Erwin W. Lutzer

Who shall separate us from the love of Christ?
Shall trouble or hardship or persecution
or famine or nakedness or danger or sword? . . .
No, in all these things we are more
than conquerors through him who loved us.
For I am convinced that neither death nor life,
neither angels nor demons, neither the present
nor the future, nor any powers, neither height
nor depth, nor anything else in all creation,
will be able to separate us from the love of God
that is in Christ Jesus our Lord.

Romans 8:35, 37–39

Live in God's Love

I n the book of Romans, the apostle Paul tells us that what should matter most to you and to me and to him is to live in the care and love of God. And nothing can threaten that. Nothing! In some mysterious way, the strength and power of Jesus Christ are available to me and you for the situations of life in which we find ourselves.

> I can do everything
> through him who gives me strength.
> Philippians 4:13

Ultimately, you are not vulnerable to any kind of enemy, because you live in the care of God. That really is the message of the gospel, if you've asked Jesus Christ to be the Lord and the Savior of your life. You live in the hand of God, whatever it is you face.

I pray that you, being rooted
and established in love, may have power,
together with all the saints,
to grasp how wide and long and high and deep
is the love of Christ, and to know
this love that surpasses knowledge—
that you may be filled to the measure
of all the fullness of God.

Ephesians 3:17-19

Keep yourselves in God's love.

Jude 21

God is love.

1 John 4:16

We recognize the nature of God best, not by thinking about his power or wisdom, which are terrifying, but by thinking about his goodness and love. Then we are truly born anew in God, and we can grow in faith.

Martin Luther

How great is the love
the Father has lavished on us,
that we should be called children of God!
And that is what we are!

1 John 3:1

Start Each Day
With God

In the morning, O LORD, you hear my voice;
in the morning I lay my requests before you
and wait in expectation.

Psalm 5:3

Make it your goal tomorrow to spend the day with Jesus. You can get so weighed down because you think everything rests on your shoulders. But it doesn't. The vast majority of things in this world you don't affect one way or the other. God makes the sun come up. God gives you air and food and all the stuff you need to live, and everybody else, too. It's God's world. And beginning the day with God reminds us of that.

The way you get up in the morning sets the tone for the rest of the day, so here's the task: Tomorrow, as soon as you can, get alone for a few minutes with God. This is very important. Don't try to be heroic with this or you'll set yourself up for failure. Don't try to make it last an hour. Five minutes is fine. Get alone, and renew your invitation from Jesus to be with you all day.

Go over your plans for the day. If you have a calendar, open it up and look over it with Jesus. As you're going through it, you'll have some concerns. Just hand them over to him. Maybe you'll notice a meeting or an appointment that you're worried about. Ask him for wisdom. Give him any burdens that you have.

So many people start their day, day after day, anxious, hurried, frenzied, fearful, afraid, or rushed. You don't have to! You're going to start your day anyway, why not start it with Jesus? Do you have any better offers? You're going to have a first thought anyhow; you're going to have a first word of the day, why not let it belong to God, before whom all anxieties and impurities and restlessness flee? You can do this. You can start each day with God.

For Christians, the beginning
of the day should not
be haunted by the various
kinds of concerns they
face during the day. The Lord
stands above the new day,
for God has made it.
All restlessness, all impurity,
all worry and anxiety flee
before him. Therefore, in the
early morning hours
of the day, may our many
thoughts and our many idle
words be silent, and may
the first word and the first
thought belong to the one to
whom our whole life belongs.

Dietrich Bonhoffer

Because of the LORD's great love we
are not consumed,
for his compassions never fail.
They are new every morning;
great is your faithfulness. . . .
The LORD is good to those whose hope is in him,
to the one who seeks him.

Lamentations 3:22–23, 25

Satisfy us in the morning, O LORD, with your
unfailing love,
that we may sing for joy and be glad all our days.

Psalm 90:14

O LORD, be gracious to us;
we long for you.
Be our strength every morning,
our salvation in time of distress.

Isaiah 33:2

Live Immersed in the
Presence of God

I have set the LORD always before me.

Psalm 16:8

The place where we must always register God's presence is in our minds, our thoughts and feelings, our inner being. That means that my job, in my spiritual life, is to learn to continually focus my attention on God. I think about him, talk to him, ask for his help, tell him my plans, pour out my heart to him, describe my problems, and give thanks for his joy. The practice of spiritual life boils down to one single statement from Scripture: "I have set the LORD always before me." This is the simplest description of spiritual life in the entire Bible.

There are certain thoughts that are characteristic of God. When these thoughts are present, there's a real good chance that they are the result of God's walking alongside of you.

The first thought involves thoughts and feelings of reassurance. It's important that you understand that whatever you do in life, God longs to partner with you. God wants to say to you, "Don't be afraid, because I'm with you."

The second thought that you will have when God is present with you, is that you'll get guidance. Maybe you're stumped with some issue, and then an idea comes to you. It might be a big one. It might be a small one, but it will help. It's just what you need. Or you're with someone else, or even a group of people, and you're about to say something stupid, something self-promotional, something that will inflict damage. All of a sudden, a little voice inside your head says, "Shut up." Where does that voice come from?

It comes from God. God is closer than you think. Every time you listen and respond, you increase your capacity for being with God. And it's a little more likely that you'll be the kind of person that God can use.

A third indicator of God's presence occurs when you're going down the wrong road and a little stab of pain says, "No, turn around." When the Spirit of God is present, he will convict the world with regard to sin and righteousness and judgment. There will be thoughts that say, "Stop going that way. Turn around. Go the other direction."

The fourth kind of thought that will tell you God is present is joy. The basic response to the presence of God is joy, because that's the kind of person God is. You can't be around him if you're healthy and right without some of that joy in his presence just spilling over into your life. Sometimes when God is present, you'll know, because a little voice inside your head will say, "Dance." Music will be playing that just makes you happy. You'll start singing and dancing and looking like a fool. It will give you joy. Maybe if you put effort in at work and something gets accomplished that's significant, you'll get a surge of satisfaction—that's a little echo of what happened when God was creating the world. When that happens, God is closer than you think.

God can use an infinite variety of ways to express his presence, because he made them all. He can use his creation, other people, Scripture, teaching, or solitude. God can use any of those things to convey his presence and character. If you set the Lord ever before you, you will come to see his presence in your ordinary, fallen life.

God is closer than you think.

God is not far from each one of us.

Acts 17:27

Be strong and courageous. Do not be terrified;
do not be discouraged, for the LORD your God
will be with you wherever you go.

Joshua 1:9

O LORD, you have made known to me
the path of life;
you will fill me with joy in your presence.

Psalm 16:11

"Surely the LORD is in this place—
and I did not know it!"

Genesis 28:16 (NRSV)

How hard is it for God to get
your attention? Do you
regularly practice turning
aside in your day?
That is, taking a moment
to listen to God—because God,
through the Holy Spirit,
really is speaking, because we
know, every place is filled
with the presence of God.
There is not an inch of space,
not a moment of time,
that God does not inhabit.

We shall never encounter God in the moment when that encounter takes place. It's always afterward that we can say, "so that strange situation, that impression, that unexplainable event was God."

Jacques Ellul

Be a Jesus
Follower

"Come, follow me," Jesus said,
"and I will make you fishers of men."
At once they left their nets and followed him.

Matthew 4:19-20

In the New Testament, the word for a fully devoted follower was the word "disciple". It means to be a student or an apprentice to someone. It was quite easy to tell if someone had done that. A disciple—like Peter, James, or John—had made a decision to spend every day with Jesus to learn how to be like him.

It's important to understand that, mostly, they did the same kinds of activities everyone else did. They ate, slept, worked, played, learned. They just did all of these things with Jesus, and they couldn't believe they had gotten to do this! They had left behind a lot— jobs, families—but they did this with great joy. They couldn't believe they had gotten this opportunity to follow Jesus.

When Jesus defeated death and was raised again to life, he said that now nothing—not even death itself—could keep his friends, his students, his disciples from being with him. Jesus' final words to his friends were, "Lo, I am with you always, even to the end of the age" (Matthew 28:20 NKJV). Always!

The risen Jesus also said, "Listen! I am standing at the door, knocking; if you hear my voice and open the door, I will come in to you" (Revelation 3:20 NRSV). Here or there, down through the centuries, someone hears and someone opens, and Jesus comes in. When that happens, something changes in this world.

I have been crucified with Christ and I no longer live, but Christ lives in me. The life I live in the body, I live by faith in the Son of God, who loved me and gave himself for me.

Galatians 2:20

And now it's your turn. What happened to Peter, James, and John on the other side of the world, 2,000 years ago, can happen again. It can happen for you if you want it to. Your age, your season of life, your temperament, your job—these are no obstacles to Jesus at all. Jesus' invitation is not just to be with you when you go to church, meet with a small group, or read the Bible. He offers to be with you in every moment of your life.

I don't care what other opportunities come your way financially, vocationally, or relationally. Throughout history, when human beings came to understand what it was that Jesus was really offering, they would sacrifice anything—their job, money, comfort, home, security—risk suffering, and do it all with joy, to get the chance to be an apprentice to Jesus, to be a Jesus-follower. This is your chance to follow him, too.

Jesus said, "Those who find their life will lose it, and those who lose their life for my sake will find it."

Matthew 10:39 (TNIV)

What does the LORD require of you?
To act justly and to love mercy
and to walk humbly with your God.

Micah 6:8

If we were willing to
learn the meaning of
real discipleship and
actually to become
disciples, the church in
the West would be
transformed, and the
resultant impact on
society would
be staggering.

David Watson

I'm part of the fellowship of the unashamed. I have the Holy Spirit power. The die has been cast. I have stepped over the line. The decision has been made—I'm a disciple of his. I won't look back, let up, slow down, back away, or be still. My past is redeemed, my present makes sense, my future is secure. I'm finished and done with low living, sight walking, smooth knees, colorless dreams, tamed visions, worldly talking, cheap giving, and dwarfed goals.

I no longer need preeminence, prosperity, position, promotions, plaudits, or popularity. I don't have to be right, first, tops, recognized, praised, regarded, or rewarded. I now live by faith, lean in his presence, walk by patience, am uplifted by prayer, and I labor with power.

A young pastor in Zimbabwe, Africa, later martyred for his faith in Christ.

Jesus said,
"Those who love me will keep my word,
and my Father will love them,
and we will come to them
and make our home with them."

John 14:23 (NRSV)

Spend Time
Alone

Solitude is fundamental. It's a crucial practice in following Christ. When Jesus would go to be alone with the Father, he would soak up God's love. And then he'd be free to abound in God's work and help people. Down through the centuries, Jesus' followers discovered that they could never have the kind of freedom that Jesus had if they didn't practice times of being alone with the Father.

When I first started to realize the importance of spending time alone with God I set a goal for myself: "I'll try to spend a whole day alone with God." So I waited for a free day to come up when I could do that.

Guess how long I waited? It never happened. And I discovered that if I was really serious about having time alone with God, I would have to schedule it.

I'd have to get out my calendar and write down, "Time alone with God," and then not let anything else infringe on it.

If you're serious about following Christ, do this: Get out your calendar and schedule it in. Don't try to be overly heroic. If you've never done something like this before, don't start with a whole day. Start with a few moments in the morning, or take a lunch hour to be with God. It won't happen if you don't make it happen. Without a consistent, steady diet of teaching from God's Word and talking and listening to him, you don't stand a chance of living your life as a disciple of Christ.

The LORD is with you when you are with him. If you seek him, he will be found by you.

2 Chronicles 15:2

Be still, and know that I am God.

Psalm 46:10

Come near to God and he will come near to you.

J a m e s   4 : 8

Jesus said to his disciples, "Come with me by your-selves to a quiet place and get some rest."

M a r k   6 : 3 1

Pray About Everything

Do not be anxious about anything, but in every-thing, by prayer and petition, with thanksgiving, present your requests to God.

Philippians 4:6

Often, when I pray, I don't talk to God about things that I'm really thinking about because they just don't sound very spiritual. So I talk to God about the things that I think sound much more spiritual (as if the only time God is monitoring what's on my mind is when I pray). So I'll pray about world peace, or world hunger, or the missionaries, or something like that. But my mind keeps wandering back to the other stuff that is really on my heart. The solution to this wandering-mind problem is contained in this phrase: "in everything." And the solution is this: I must pray *what is in me,* not what *I wish was in me.*

Praying what is really in my heart is an "in everything" kind of prayer. I don't wait to clean up my motives first. I don't try to sound more spiritual than I am. I don't pray what I think ought to be in me, or what I think God wants to hear. I pray what's really in me.

> "Before they call I will answer;
> while they are still speaking I will hear."
> Isaiah 65:24

Richard Foster talks about this as "simple prayer," the most common kind of prayer in the Bible. You just have to talk to God about whatever is on your heart. That is simple prayer. You pray to God not about what you think ought to be in you, but about what really is in you, about the desires of your heart. And if you're going to grow in prayer and overcome worry, you must begin by becoming an "in everything" prayer.

Start today. Pray what is in you, not what you wish was in you. Whether your request is large or small, whether your motives are mixed or pure, whether what you ask is wise or foolish, God can sort all that out.

You can trust him to respond wisely. He's not going to give you something foolishly. But you've got to learn to hold your prayer loosely and trust that if God doesn't answer it the way that you want it to be answered, he has very good reasons. He's very wise.

Your job is to talk to God about what is really on your heart. So become an "in everything" pray-er.

This is the confidence we have
in approaching God: that if we ask
anything according to his will, he hears us.

1 John 5:14

I have been driven many times to my knees by the overwhelming conviction that I had nowhere else to go.

Abraham Lincoln

"For I know the plans I have for you," declares the LORD, "plans to prosper you and not to harm you, plans to give you hope and a future. Then you will call upon me and come and pray to me, and I will listen to you. You will seek me and find me when you seek me with all your heart."

Jeremiah 29:11-13

To be a Christian
without prayer is no
more possible than to
be alive without
breathing.

Martin Luther

Pray continually.
1 Thessalonians 5:17

God insists that
we ask, not because
He needs to know our
situation, but because
we need the spiritual
discipline of asking.

Catherine Marshall

To be a disciple of Jesus is quite a simple thing, and you really can do it! You just go through life saying, "What is the one thing needed in this moment, right here?" And if you're not exactly sure at any moment what that one needed thing is, then just pray and make the best choice you can.

At the end of the day, the world will turn out to have been made up of two kinds of people: people whose ultimate goal is to hear and do the Word of God, and people whose ultimate goal is anything else.

It's such a simple thing to go through a day asking God, "What's the one thing needed that you have for me in this moment?" And then you need to do it. Whoever you are, whatever your job, whatever your background, starting right this moment, you can do it. Ask and pray.

Trust and Obey

The LORD is good, a refuge in times of trouble.
He cares for those who trust in him.

Nahum 1:7

Over and over, we say these words to children: "Don't be afraid." The point of this statement is not primarily to comfort. The point of God's saying it over and over again to his people throughout the Bible (and he does so over twenty times) is not primarily to comfort them, or to tell them to just be comfortable and go through life without anxiety. No, the point of it is: "Take action. Don't let your fear keep you from responding in obedience." The primary point is not that you will never experience anxiety, because as you're going through life, very often you'll receive a new directive, and in order to respond in faith, you'll have to face your fear all over again.

But once you take the action and obey, you put yourself in the position where your faith can grow. You don't need faith that has no doubts; you just need enough to respond to God in obedience. And when you do respond, you put yourself in the place where you can discover that God really is faithful. But if you don't take the step of obedience, you'll never know his great faithfulness.

God says, "Fear not. Jump in. Go to the promised land. Believe me even though it's frightening. Obey me even though it's frightening. And you will come to discover that I can be trusted."

It's a hard thing to obey when fear creeps into your life. It's an issue of trust. My challenge to you is this: Take some area in which you are afraid but in which you know God is calling you to respond in faith.

Don't let fear hold you back. Trust God. Obey God.

Trust in the LORD with all your heart
and lean not on your own understanding;
in all your ways acknowledge him,
and he will make your paths straight.

Proverbs 3:5-6

You will keep in perfect peace
him whose mind is steadfast,
because he trusts in you.
Trust in the LORD forever,
for the LORD, the LORD, is the Rock eternal.

Isaiah 26:3-4

Do not merely listen to the word. . . .
Do what it says.

James 1:22

Stop
Hiding

Then the man and his wife heard the sound of the
LORD God as he was walking in the garden in
the cool of the day, and they hid from the LORD
God among the trees of the garden. But the
LORD God called to the man, "Where are you?"

Genesis 3:8–9

One of the most amazing, gracious, humble things about God is that he wants so much to be in a freely chosen, love relationship with human beings that he will allow us to hide from him if we want to. But think about that for a moment. This is God, who is omniscient—there is nothing he does not know. He is omnipresent—there's not one square inch of the universe that he does not occupy. Is trying to hide from God a real smart strategy?

God says, "Hey, son, hey, daughter, where are you? Won't you just come to me? Won't you just tell me everything?" You need to know that God promises to accept you fully, to forgive you utterly.

Our part is to stop hiding. Just come out and say, "All right, God, I'm going to tell you everything. I'm going to pour my heart out to you—all the good and all the bad—and I'll receive your forgiveness and your acceptance as a gift of grace."

To anyone who does this, to anyone who receives the gift of forgiveness, God says, "Come home. I know all about you. I love you. I'll walk with you through this life, and be with you for all of eternity. You're fully known. You're fully loved."

The LORD your God is with you,
he is mighty to save.
He will take great delight in you,
he will quiet you with his love,
he will rejoice over you with singing.

Zephaniah 3:17

At the creation
of the world,
God had this dream.
It was a dream
of community,
a community of
loving persons.
That's what the world
was to be.

Stay Connected

God created you for community. You were made for relational connectedness. You were designed by God to love and be loved; to know and be known; to serve and be served; to celebrate and be celebrated.

> The Lord God said, "It is not good for the man to be alone. I will make a helper suitable for him."
>
> Genesis 2:18

To miss out on this is to miss out on the reason why God made you. Whatever else you achieve in life—whatever else you accomplish, however much stuff you pile up, however high you climb the corporate ladder, if you miss this, you miss the reason why you were made. Without deep relational connectedness, you cannot have fullness of life. More importantly, without deep relational connectedness, you cannot know and serve God.

Inside every human being, there is a God-shaped void—and a human-shaped one, as well—that nothing else can fill. There is no substitute that will fill this need in you for human relationship, for community—not money, not achievement, not busyness, not books.

Community, deep connectedness with God and with people, is what you were made for. It is God's design and desire for your life. It is the one indispensable condition for human growth.

I can survive without a lot
of things, but to live
without friends would be
to live in a cave and never
see the sunrise again.
We need the input,
the challenge,
the encouragement,
even the "spur" that comes
from others in community.
We call on each other
to celebrate, and we call on
each other to weep.
Surely this is a treasure
above others, a piece
of heaven, a promise of
what is to come.

Sheila Walsh

Join a Church
Group

There is nothing in the world like being part of a little band, a community sitting around a little circle, devoted together to a mission, a cause, devoted to building the kingdom of Christ, and deeply devoted to each other. There is nothing in the world like that rich community. You tell stories and you dream dreams, because behind every name and every face around that circle, is a story and a dream. I'll tell you, friends, when you get to the end of your life, to have been a part of a circle like that will be the greatest treasure you've ever known. You will have known deep intimacy. You will have had the grand adventure of contributing to the greatest cause in the history of the earth—the building of the kingdom of God. You will have been a part of a story bigger than yourself.

I hope you're a part of a little group like this. If you're not, get in one. Become part of a community.

> **The closer we are to God, the closer we are to those who are close to him.**
>
> Thomas Merton

Choose to
Serve Others

The secret to abundant living is creative, joyful, freely chosen servanthood. You will receive more than you expect when you give more than is required. When you just try to get by, you will just get by. When you give and then some, you will receive and then some. This won't necessarily be in terms of material resources, but it is certainly true in terms of life, joy, and character. You will live and then some.

Jesus said, "Whoever wants to become great among you must be your servant, and whoever wants to be first must be your slave—just as the Son of Man did not come to be served, but to serve, and to give his life as a ransom for many."

Matthew 20:26–28

Be devoted to one another in brotherly love.
Honor one another above yourselves.
Never be lacking in zeal,
but keep your spiritual fervor,
serving the Lord.

Romans 12:10-11

Practice Diversity

There is neither Jew nor Greek, slave nor free, male
nor female, for you are all one in Christ Jesus.

Galatians 3:28

Our God, the God of the Bible, is an equal-opportunity God. His love knows no boundaries or barriers—not of race, not of gender, not of socioeconomic status. He is unalterably committed to tearing down the walls that we erect to separate ourselves from others.

Refuse to let yourself be isolated. One of the most powerful things you can do is to cultivate significant relationships with people from diverse backgrounds. And as you relate to people that have a different accent or a different skin color, or are from another culture, or have various kinds of physical or mental challenges, be open to these people. Don't exclude them from your heart. Treat them the way that Jesus would treat them.

Peter began to speak: "I now realize how
true it is that God does not show favoritism but
accepts those from every nation
who fear him and do what is right."

Acts 10:34–35 (TNIV)

Be wise in the way you act toward outsiders;
make the most of every opportunity.

Colossians 4:5

Show proper respect to everyone.

1 Peter 2:17

Understanding and
accepting diversity
enables us to see that
each of us is needed.
It also enables us to
begin to think about
being abandoned
to the strengths of
others, of admitting
that we cannot know
or do everything.

Max De Pree

Gather Together
In Worship

Jesus said, "Where two or three come together in my name, there am I with them."

Matthew 18:20

It is so important that you arrange your life around the gathering together of Christians. It's not because God is taking attendance, and this is some way of showing him how committed you are. It's because you and I need it if we are going to live with purpose. For one thing, we need it to keep our hearts from growing cold to the things of God. There is something that happens when people come together to worship and to learn.

A few years ago we were on vacation at a little cabin on a lake. As usual, I grilled dinner several nights that week out on a Weber barbecue grill. My son was going through a stage in which he was just fascinated by fire—a typical developmental stage for boys that starts at about age five and lasts fifty or sixty years. I started the fire, and he watched it all very closely. I poured on the lighter fluid, and he kept encouraging me to pour on more and more and more and more. And then, as you may know, we had to put those little charcoal briquettes close together to get a really hot fire.

It's a weird thing about briquettes—if they're isolated and scattered, the fire goes out. Something happens to all those little briquettes when they're together that doesn't happen when they're alone. It's the way God made briquettes.

That's the same way God made the human heart. It just is. Ignore the fact or defy it at your own peril. The human heart needs closeness and fellowship to stay on fire. This is the fellowship of the burning heart. You are not going to have a heart that blazes with the presence of Jesus if you're in isolation. You're just not. As the evil one knows so well, scatter the flock and hearts grow cold. Neglect the practice of assembling for worship and learning, and the fire starts to fade. But gather the body together and something happens—Jesus is there.

Commit yourself to practicing the discipline of assembly. Don't let it drift. Don't neglect it. It's not because God is taking attendance, but because you get inundated every day of your life with the counsel of the ungodly. Your mind and your soul need to be in the presence of brothers and sisters worshiping and listening to God.

Cultivate
Friendships

Devote yourselves, with God's help, to cultivating great, life-changing, heart-shaping, character-forming friends.

If you want deep friendship, you cannot always be the strong one. And in our world, that could be kind of scary. But you let a friend see you in your weakness. You open yourself to them. Some of you have never done this, and you wonder why you're lonely. You're going to have to get vulnerable to have a friend. Now, you can't do this all at once. You have to be wise about it. You have to build trust over time. But if you really want a deep friendship, you cannot live with deep secrets.

Friends serve each other. Sometimes they're not think-ing about themselves, they're thinking about their friend. Friends do that. When's the last time you performed an extraordinary act of servanthood for the well-being of a friend to whom you're devoted? A friend is someone that you commit to, not because of what they can do for you, not because they're useful to you, but just because they're your friend.

Friends listen, really listen, even though they're busy. Listening is an act of humility and love. Listening says, *I'm going to put my own agenda on the shelf, and I'm going to devote myself to knowing you.* Friends are not generally looking for someone who can talk very impressively or cleverly or with great wit. Mostly, what people are looking for is a world-class listener.

When something goes right, friends raise the roof. Do you do that with your friends? When's the last time your friends had God bless them—had something go right in their life and you threw a party? Or wrote them a three-page letter telling them what they mean to you? Sent them a gift? Jumped up and down with glee over what God has done for them?

Our whole vision is to be a biblically authentic community—to live in friendship with God and friendship with each other. And if you're not in that kind of friendship right now, you can't make it happen, but you can open yourself up to it. You can start pursuing it. You can start praying. You can ask God to guide you. You can take little relational risks with somebody in your life. And if you have friends like that, you should prize them, cherish them, and take that friendship as deep as you can.

*Some friends play at friendship
but a true friend sticks closer than one's nearest kin.*

Proverbs 18:24 (NRSV)

*Two are better than one, because they have a
good reward for their toil. For if they fall, one will
lift up the other; but woe to one who is alone and
falls and does not have another to help.*

Ecclesiastes 4:9–10 (NRSV)

It is not possible
to live a rich, full life
without friends.
I have to be one to
have one.

Anne Wilson Schaef

Pray

Pray for people. Talk to God about people. And when you get a leading to call somebody, to write somebody a note, to encourage somebody, to wrap your arms around somebody, don't blow it off. This is your chance to love the people who mean so much to God. Remember how short life is and what really matters. It's all about love.

Do Small Things

Sometimes we spend years waiting for guidance from God for the real big things—a really important job, maybe, or the right marriage, or a big, financial deal. We get so preoccupied with "me." Sometimes we're willing to spend a fair amount of energy and time and effort to do something that will look big, or impressive, or splashy. But how do you respond when God asks you to do something small? What would it be like if we just served each other in small ways?

Mostly God calls people just to do small things: listen to a child, help somebody at work, pray for somebody in trouble, do an errand for somebody at home, encourage somebody who's a little discouraged, be patient when we're standing in line, or notice the person who busses our table and say a little prayer of blessing for them.

Mother Teresa once said, "God doesn't ask us to do great things. He asks us to do small things with great love."

This service that you perform is not only supplying the needs of God's people but is also overflowing in many expressions of thanks to God.
2 Corinthians 9:12

Share with God's people who are in need. Practice hospitality.
Romans 12:13

When asked what we ought to do in the world, Jesus said that we should love one another. Each day we have a personal opportunity to be like Jesus and bridge the gap between ourselves and others.

Do not forget to do good and to share with others, for with such sacrifices God is pleased.
Hebrews 13:16

Perhaps there is some-
one you dislike but
whom you have to see
each day. What would
happen if you sent
that person a small
card of greeting?
What would happen if
you invited that
person out for a cup
of coffee? What would
happen if you bought
that person a flower?
God would smile.
That's what
would happen.

Christopher de Vinck

Thank God
For Sex!

God created humankind in his image,
in the image of God he created them;
male and female he created them.

Genesis 1:27 (NRSV)

God made human beings as male and female and created sex! So accept and be grateful that God made you to be a sexual person. You may have problems handling it, but you must not despise what God has done.

Sex was not some great mistake God made when he ran out of good ideas. Eve was brought to Adam, and Adam's response was not, "I'll bet she's got a wonderful personality!"

Remember what Adam said? "This now is bone of my bones and flesh of my flesh. Hooray, God!" is what Adam said.

But when people don't understand God's original intent, tragic things happen. God does not want to destroy your ability to see and experience your sexuality. He wants to redeem it.

You should not despise God's gift, your body. You need to be grateful for that gift. You need to get to the point where you can say honestly, "Thanks, God, that you made me with a body. Thanks that you made me male (or female). Thanks that you gave the human race the capacity for oneness within the covenant of marriage." That last part is very important because God has ordained that a sexual relationship be reserved for the covenant of marriage.

Righteousness, as Jesus defines it, is not simply the avoidance of sin. Of course, you shouldn't put yourself in a position in which you know you're going to be sexually tempted. But the ultimate goal, what Jesus wants us to become, is the kind of person that can look at a person of the opposite sex and see what Jesus sees.

If that's not your spouse or a person that you're romantically involved with, you'll see a brother or a sister. And when you extend a hand, you'll touch and embrace as Jesus would touch and embrace. That's what righteousness is.

If we live by the Spirit,
let us also be guided by the Spirit.
Galatians 5:25 (NRSV)

Flee from sexual immorality. All other sins
people commit are outside their bodies,
but those who sin sexually sin against their own
bodies. Do you not know that your bodies are
temples of the Holy Spirit, who is in you,
whom you have received from God?
You are not your own; you were bought at
a price. Therefore honor God with your bodies.
1 Corinthians 6:18–20 (TNIV)

All that is in the world—the desire of the flesh,
the desire of the eyes, the pride in riches—
comes not from the Father but from the world.
And the world and its desire are passing away,
but those who do the will of God live forever.
1 John 2:16–17 (NRSV)

Sex is not sin.
Sex is not salvation,
either. Like
nitroglycerin, it can
be used either
to blow up bridges
or heal hearts.

Frederick Buechner

Save Sex
For Marriage

It is God's will that you should be sanctified:
that you should avoid sexual immorality;
that each of you should learn to control your own
body in a way that is holy and honorable.

1 Thessalonians 4:3-4 (TNIV)

Make a commitment to keep God's standards and restrict a sexual relationship for the permanent commitment of marriage.

God intended sex for a husband and a wife who have committed themselves to each other permanently, because it is only in the context of a permanent commitment that that level of intimacy can be safely expressed. When there's an ultimate expression of physical intimacy, but there's not a permanent commitment, somebody's going to get hurt.

Now, you and I need to make the resolution to keep ourselves pure and follow God's directives. We need to make it now. We need to make it before we get into situations in which we're going to be tempted to break it, because if we wait until then, we've waited too long. We're not going to make it then! The pressure to go against God's standards is so intense in our society that if we have not decided ahead of time to hold to them, it's not going to happen.

We live in a society in which it is countercultural to say, "I will not be sexually active. I will reserve a sexual relationship for marriage, when and if I should ever get married."

We all struggle to be sexually right and pursue right-eousness. Sexuality is such a deep part of us. And guilt about sex has a way of making people feel separated from God like nothing else. So you need to pledge to live with sexual integrity and purity. You need to make the commitment: "I'm not going to allow my sin to keep me from God. I'm going to chose to keep God's standards. I'm going to rely on his Spirit to give me strength day by day, and whenever I do sin, I'm going to get right back up and cling to God."

"Haven't you read," Jesus replied, "that at the beginning the Creator 'made them male and female,' and said, 'For this reason a man will leave his father and mother and be united to his wife, and the two will become one flesh'? So they are no longer two, but one. Therefore what God has joined together, let no one separate."

Matthew 19:4–6 (TNIV)

The greatest sign
of a spiritually mature human
being is not a head crammed
with knowledge—although
that's not necessarily a bad
thing—but the greatest sign of a
spiritually mature human
being is a heart that desperately
loves people, desperately loves
Jesus, and desperately wants
to bring them together.

Live for God's Approval

Am I now trying to win the approval of men,
or of God? Or am I trying to please men?
If I were still trying to please men,
I would not be a servant of Christ.

Galatians 1:10

Living in the love of God, living in the gracious acceptance and approval of God, will liberate you from the "approval addiction"—living in bondage to what other people think about you. When you are addicted, no matter how much of your drug of choice you get, you never have enough. You've got to have more and more and more fixes, and like other junkies, you go crazy when this drug—the approval of others—is withheld. When you are an approval addict, you are always vulnerable to other people's opinions about you, and your life becomes an emotional roller coaster.

The apostle Paul, to a large extent, was liberated from

this approval addition, because he lived in the com-mendation of God. He was free to speak the truth in love. He was free to confront when people needed to be confronted, and he was free to be gentle when people needed gentleness. He could defy people or even confront them with great boldness when he needed to, because he didn't fear their disapproval. If they told Paul they didn't like him, he wasn't devastated. He didn't fall apart. His life was not built on their approval. Paul lived under the approval of God; his style was to be humble and gentle. He didn't go around comparing himself with other people or trying to demonstrate his superiority. He didn't need to impress people. He didn't need to be the one who was always in charge. He didn't need to be in competition with other people or to be flashy. Paul lived a different kind of life than his opponents, and that enabled him to live under the approval of God and to be liberated from the need to seek approval from other people.

Someone once said, "When you are in your twenties, you live to please other people. When you're in your thirties, you get tired of trying to please other people, and you get mad at them. When you're in your forties, you realize nobody was thinking about you the whole time anyhow."

The truth is that generally, other people are too busy worrying about what you are thinking about them to think anything about you. It's just not wise to live to please others, because once you get on that track, you're on a treadmill, and no matter how fast you run, you're never going to get anywhere. You're trying to feed an appetite that will be absolutely insatiable.

To live in the kingdom of God means to have freedom from the oppressive burden of having to worry about other people's opinions. What gives us the strength to deal with criticism and conflict is that we are very clear about our identity, and our identity is this: We belong to Christ. And if we belong to Christ, what else really matters?

Give up the whole business of trying to convince people how smart you are, or how successful you are, or how clever you are, or how attractive you are. Just give it up, friends. Instead, live in the acceptance and the approval of our God, who is wonderful beyond words.

Just as we have been approved by God
to be entrusted with the message of the gospel,
even so we speak, not to please mortals,
but to please God who tests our hearts.
1 Thessalonians 2:4 (NRSV)

Do your best to present yourself
to God as one approved, a worker who
does not need to be ashamed and
who correctly handles the word of truth.

2 Timothy 2:15 (TNIV)

If we live, we live to the Lord; and if we die,
we die to the Lord. So, whether we live or die,
we belong to the Lord.

Romans 14:8

To truly care for people requires not caring too much about their approval or their disapproval.

Watch Your

Temper

A fool gives full vent to anger,
but the wise quietly holds it back.
Proverbs 29:11 (NRSV)

Anger does not produce God's righteousness. Human anger, unless it is managed and expressed with great skill, tends to have unintended consequences. Some of us need to be slow to speak, especially when we're angry. Or some of us mismanage our anger by becoming cold and distant and withdrawing from the person who made us angry. In either case, we need to manage our anger differently.

Life is too short, and intimacy and community are too precious, for us to get to the end of our lives and regret that we never learned to handle our anger in a right, God-honoring way.

Resolve right now that when you get angry, you will

not flip into "default mode." Think before you respond. If you tend to blow up, pause and think and then respond calmly. If you tend to avoid needed confrontation, pause and swallow deep and then have the courage to speak the truth in love. Confrontation may be hard, and it may even be easier to simply stay angry, but that is not what God calls us to do.

A gentle answer turns away wrath,
but a harsh word stirs up anger.
Proverbs 15:1

People who give themselves to relational greatness–people who have deep friends whom they laugh with and cry with, with whom they learn together, with whom they fight and forgive, with whom they dance and grow and live and die–these are the human beings who lead magnificent lives, whether or not they are ever noted in society. And when they die, not one of them regrets having devoted them-selves to people–to their friends, to their children, to their family–not one.

livingthegoodlife.com

You've hardly even
started your life.
The gun is just going
off. Your race is only
beginning. The whole
adventure lies before
you. Friends, your real
work hasn't even
started yet. You have
no idea what your
potential is.

living on
Purpose

The LORD will fulfill his purpose for me;
your love, O LORD, endures forever—
do not abandon the works of your hands.

Psalm 138:8

You can live by default, or you can live on purpose. You can let the world squeeze you into its mold, or you can be formed by the thoughts of God.

Nobody sits down and plans to lead a mediocre life. No couple getting married plans to get a divorce. Nobody walks into a bar and plans to become an alcoholic. No one has kids and plans on being so busy that the kids grow up to be strangers.

Nobody nurses a grudge and plans on becoming a bitter, resentful person. No one "gets religion" and plans to become judgmental and self-righteous. Nobody plans to go to hell. It just happens.

Given our inner condition of fallenness, the outer condition of the world, and the fact that we live in that sinful world, fallenness is such a pervasive way of life that, really, the alternative must be radical. Standard operating procedure with a smattering of religious activities mixed in is not going to get transformation done.

You will have to live by design and on purpose. You will have to deliberately allow God to transform your way of thinking and feeling as you saturate yourself in God's mind and God's heart.

You will have to live on purpose.

We know that in all things God works for the good of those who love him, who have been called according to his purpose.

Romans 8:28

Good morning, God. I love you! What are you up to today? I want to be a part of it.

Norman Grubb

We continually remember before our God and Father your work produced by faith, your labor prompted by love, and your endurance inspired by hope in our Lord Jesus Christ.

1 Thessalonians 1:3

Periods of staleness
in life are not inevitable,
but they are common.
We can keep from going
stale by getting
proper rest, by practicing
complete candor in
prayer, by introducing
variety into our lives,
by heeding God's call
to move onward,
and by exercising
quiet faith always.

A. W. Tozer

sing

Sing and make music in your heart to the Lord.

Ephesians 5:19

Singing strengthens the soul somehow. Singing forms us. So, be a singing person. When you gather with others, sing for all you're worth.

Sing alone. Get a worship tape. Play it in your car. Play it when you're home, or use it in your devotional life. Sing sometimes just for you and God. Sing to him.

Some of you may have great voices. Some of you may not be able to carry a tune in a bucket. It doesn't matter. It brings joy to the heart of God when his children sing to him. Devote yourself to it.

Praise the LORD.
How good it is to sing praises to our God,
how pleasant and fitting to praise him!

Psalm 147:1

Don't Judge

Jesus said, "Do not judge, or you too will be judged. For in the same way you judge others, you will be judged, and with the measure you use, it will be measured to you."

Matthew 7:1-2

Make it your firm intention and practice not to condemn anyone in thought, word, or deed. Really. Refrain from gossip—even when it's couched subtly enough so that you could get away with it. Even when you're with a "safe" person whom you know would join in the gossip with you. Be patient with people who are not living up to your high standards. Don't judge.

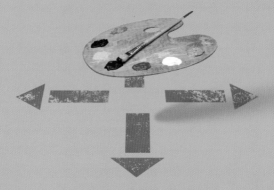

Joy is the serious business of heaven.

C. S. Lewis

Be Joyful

Be joyful always.
1 Thessalonians 5:16

God loves to express joy. Joy lives in the very heart of God. Joy is the gift to people who live in God's heart.

You will not understand about God until you understand this about him: God is the happiest being in all the universe. Joy is God's basic character. Joy is God's eternal destiny. And joy is God's desire for the human race. Joy is God's desire for you.

What I'm trying to establish here is that it's okay to be joyful! It's okay to pursue joy. It's more than okay. In fact, I give you permission to pursue joy. The joy that the Bible commands is in the framework of a Christ-honoring life. "The joy of the Lord" is joy that's experienced in a life where Christ is Lord.

You can become a joyful person. With God's help, it really is possible. It is a learned skill. The Bible would not command it if it were not so. But here's the truth: You must take responsibility for your joy—it isn't caused by your friend, your boss, your parents, or your loved ones. Your joy is your responsibility.

The question is: When are you going to practice joy? If it's a wonderful thing and if it's commanded of us, when will you practice it? Psalm 118:24 puts it like this: "This is the day the LORD has made; let us rejoice and be glad in it." When are you going to practice joy? Today!

The psalmist says this because we live in a world with the illusion that we'll be happy "someday" when the conditions in our lives change for the better. People are in school, and they think, I'll be happy someday when I graduate. People are single, and they think, I'll be happy someday when I get married. And on and on.

But this is God's day. Today is the day God made. This is the day God has redeemed in Jesus. If you're going to be joyful, it must be today. The call to joy is a call to rejoice in this day. Here's how:

1. Hang Around Joyful People.

There are people in your world who have rejected joy, who have decided to become victims. They don't want joy, and they don't want you to be joyful, either. They are "black holes" of joy, and if you give them the power, they will suck the joy right out of you. Don't hang around with them. Hang around with joyful people.

2. Practice the Discipline of Celebration.

Set aside a day a week to be a day of celebration. Fill that day with things that will bring you joy. Eat foods you love to eat. Listen to music you love to hear. Wear clothes that make you happy.

3. Find the Right Rhythm of Challenge and Rest.

All creatures are created by God with the need to be challenged. If life is too easy, it'll kill you. It sounds strange, I know, but it's true. Find a level where your life's work will stretch you and call forth your best, but where it is realistically doable, given your gifts and your temperament. Find the level of manageable difficulty.

4. Discipline Your Mind to View Life from a Biblical Perspective.

Certain kinds of thinking will lead you into joy, and certain kinds of thinking will defeat your joy.

Joy is possible, even in a desperately pain-filled world, because at the end of the story, God will dance with his people and joy will reign unblemished and uninterrupted.

You have made known to me the paths of life;
you will fill me with joy in your presence.

Acts 2:28

"This day is sacred to our Lord. Do not grieve,
for the joy of the LORD is your strength."

Nehemiah 8:10

Rejoice in the Lord always.
I will say it again: Rejoice!

Philippians 4:4

The surest mark of a Christian is not faith, or even love, but joy.

Samuel M. Shoemaker

This is the
secret of joy.
We shall no longer
strive for our
own way; but commit
ourselves, easily
and simply, to God's
way, acquiesce in his
will, and in so doing
find our peace.

Evelyn Underhill

Get Enough

Sleep

In vain you rise early and stay up late,
toiling for food to eat—
for he grants sleep to those he loves.

Psalm 127:2

Sleep is a gift from God.

We live in a world where, experts say, we have a sleep debt that is bigger than the national debt. William Dements, an expert in the study of sleep, cites research that estimates, 24,000 people die every year in car accidents caused by sleep deprivation and fatigue. This statistic staggers me! Twenty-four thousand people die every year just because we have gotten used to living in such an exhausted way. We get used to it—and we often get kind of proud of it.

Lack of sleep causes people to argue with spouses and friends, do sub-par work in their jobs, be less loving and more irritable, and generally feel miserable. It's a very hard thing to live like Jesus if you're sleep-deprived. To some of you, the single most spiritual thing that you could do is get a really good night's sleep.

Here are some concrete suggestions:

1. Arrange to have enough time tonight to sleep adequately so that you'll be rested tomorrow.
2. Avoid coffee, food, or exercise right before bedtime.
3. Don't watch TV until late into the night.
4. End your night by talking to God. Thank him for the day, and invite him to be with you tomorrow.
5. As you're putting your head on the pillow, tell God, "I'm looking forward to tomorrow. I want you to be with me all day."

You can do this. It doesn't take some kind of a spiritual super-athlete. You're going to go to sleep, anyhow—just do it in Jesus' name.

Sleep is a surrender, a laying down of arms. Whatever plans you're making, whatever work you're up to your ears in, whatever pleasures you're enjoying, whatever sorrows or anxieties or problems you're in the midst of, you set them aside, find a place to stretch out somewhere, close your eyes, and wait for sleep.

Frederick Buechner

I lie down and sleep;
I wake again, because the LORD sustains me.

I will lie down and sleep in peace,
for you alone, O LORD,
make me dwell in safety.

Psalm 4:8

When you lie down, you will not be afraid;
when you lie down, your sleep will be sweet.

Proverbs 3:24

Don't
Worry

Jesus said, "Do not worry about tomorrow,
for tomorrow will worry about itself.
Each day has enough trouble of its own."

Matthew 6:34

Worry is a huge part of our ordinary days. But the secret to actually walking with God is that you've got to learn to do it one day at a time—just one day.

God gave food, in the form of manna, to the Israelites when they were in the desert. He provided them with manna one day at a time as a kind of a picture, a faith lesson for all of us. He was saying to them, "I'll take care of you. You get so worried about stuff. I'll take care of you. I'll provide for your needs. I'll do this every day, but just one day at a time. If you get all heated up about tomorrow and start trying to hoard manna, it will spoil overnight. Tomorrow I'll give you manna for tomorrow. Today I'll give you manna for today."

God's presence is exactly like that. He will give you what you need. He will take care of you. You can depend on him, but you'll have to learn to live with him one day at a time. God will be with you for today. Tomorrow he will be with you for tomorrow. So don't worry.

Do not be anxious about anything,
but in everything, by prayer and petition, with
thanksgiving, present your requests to God.

Philippians 4:6

Cast all your anxiety on him
because he cares for you.

1 Peter 5:7

Jesus said to his disciples, "Do not worry about your life, what you will eat; or about your body, what you will wear. Life is more than food, and the body more than clothes."

Luke 12:22–23

It helps to write down half a dozen things which are worrying me. Two of them, say, disappear; about two nothing can be done, so it's no use worrying; and two perhaps can be settled.

Winston Churchill

Eat in
Joy

Go, eat your food with gladness,
and drink your wine with a joyful heart, for it is
now that God favors what you do.

Ecclesiastes 9:7

Every time you eat, whether you sit down at the table, or stand at the kitchen counter, or eat on the run, remember that food is a gift from God. Jesus told us to pray for our daily bread, because God provides. Ecclesiastes 9:7 tells us to eat our bread with joy. Do you do that?

I know, some of you are on a low-carb diet, and you're not supposed to eat bread, but you can still eat protein bars with joy! Whatever you eat, eat it with joy. Make mealtimes an exercise in gratitude. Just stop for a moment and notice what you're eating.

We live in a world where people get so rushed, they just wolf their food down. They eat so fast they don't even know they've eaten. Don't do that. When you eat, chew, and stop, and think what a good thing it is that God is providing for you.

Think Excellent Thoughts

Whatever is true, whatever is noble, whatever is right, whatever is pure, whatever is lovely, whatever is admirable—if anything is excellent or praiseworthy—think about such things.

Philippians 4:8

It's a funny thing. If you were to get the greatest performance car in the world, decide that you were going to take a serious run at the Indy 500, and dedicate yourself to winning that race, what are the odds that you would fill it with unleaded, low-octane gasoline from a thrifty discount service station? Not very high.

Or imagine that you were really serious about competing in the New York marathon and you found out you had a real shot at winning it. This becomes the all-consuming goal of your life. How likely is it that you would go on an all-Twinkies diet between now and the big event?

We're really aware that the fuel that goes into the things that matter to us ultimately determines their performance and their well-being. We're very aware of that, which is why it is so ironic to me that in the most important area of life, we disregard this one basic piece of wisdom. That area involves your mind. What you feed everything else with is nothing compared to the importance of what you feed your mind.

This is the truth that will transform your life: Think excellent thoughts.

Your mind will think most about what it is most exposed to. What enters your mind repeatedly occupies your mind, eventually shapes your mind, and ultimately expresses itself in what you do and who you become. That's the law of exposure, and this law is as inevitable and inviolable as the law of gravity.

Your mind will reflect the environment in which you stick it. It will absorb and reflect whatever it is exposed to. The events you attend, the materials that you read or don't read, the music that you listen to, the images you watch, the conversations that you hold, the daydreams that you entertain, these are all shaping your mind, eventually your character, and ultimately your destiny.

If you think that you are immune to the law of exposure and that you can just expose your mind to whatever kind of rot is in our society and have it not affect you, you are deceived.

"For my thoughts are not your thoughts, neither are your ways my ways," declares the LORD.

Isaiah 55:8

Go to God and say, "God, most of all, what I want is a new mind because I'm tired of the old one. I'm tired of how it leads me down paths toward destructiveness and foolishness and death. And in a world where messages are so often twisted or trivial or silly or foolish or self-absorbed or downright evil, I'd love to have the kind of mind that is filled with excellent, admirable, honorable, praiseworthy thoughts."

Can you image what our world would be like if we all thought that way?

Do not conform any longer to the pattern
of this world, but be transformed by the renewing
of your mind. Then you will be able to test
and approve what God's will is—
his good, pleasing and perfect will.

Romans 12:2

Set your minds on things above,
not on earthly things.

Colossians 3:2

Research has shown
that one's thought life
influences every aspect of
one's being. Kind people
are simply the type
of people who habitually
tend to think kind thoughts.
Angry people are simply
the kind of people
who habitually tend
to think thoughts that breed
resentment and hostility.

Archibald D. Hart

Read a
Book

Turn off the TV and read a book. Your mind needs that, because one of the things that happens when you turn off the TV is you will create space for your mind to have other experiences. Read a book that will really stretch your mind and cause you to think noble and honorable thoughts about what's true about God.

Reading not only enlarges and challenges the mind; it also engages and exercises the brain. Today's youth who sits mesmerized by a television screen is not going to be tomorrow's leader. Television watching is passive. Reading is active.

Richard M. Nixon

Hang On

As servants of God we commend
ourselves in every way: in great endurance;
in troubles, hardships and distresses.

2 Corinthians 6:4

Hold fast to your faith. Don't quit. God is at work in and through your sufferings in ways you cannot see and may not understand. There is a deeper music to your life than you know. Just keep going. Don't quit. Don't stop. Don't give up.

Sometimes the greatest spiritual victories on this planet are won by people who simply endure. If you can just hold on to Christ through this life with full integrity and sincerity, you are what the Bible calls an "overcomer."

At its heart, the call to endure is the call to follow Christ, and then by extension, it is to hold fast to those commitments that you must honor if you're going to be an authentic Christ-follower.

One thing to understand: God is at work in ways you cannot see.

One thing to do: Don't quit. Hang on. Keep playing. Endure.

> We work hard with our own hands.
> When we are cursed, we bless;
> when we are persecuted, we endure it.
>
> 1 Corinthians 4:12

> We also rejoice in our sufferings, because
> we know that suffering produces perseverance;
> perseverance, character; and character, hope.
> And hope does not disappoint us,
> because God has poured out his love into
> our hearts by the Holy Spirit, whom he has given us.
>
> Romans 5:3–5

One of the most tragic
things I know about
human nature is that
all of us tend to
put off living. We are
all dreaming of some
magical rose garden
over the horizon-
instead of enjoying the
roses that are
blooming outside
our windows today.

Dale Carnegie

All moments are key
moments and
life itself is grace.

Frederick Beuchner

Do What Needs
to Be Done—Now!

Anyone, then, who knows the right thing to do
and fails to do it, commits sin.

James 4:17 (NRSV)

The most dangerous word in the English language is the word "someday." *Someday* I'll quit complaining and learn to be grateful. *Someday* I'll get really serious about prayer. *Someday* I'll learn more about the Bible. *Someday* I'm going to get organized.

People can live their whole lives waiting for someday: someday when I graduate, someday when I get a job, someday when I get married, someday when we have kids. Someday I'll stop waiting and start living.

Start living now. You need to fully occupy every moment—the big, obviously dramatic ones, and the small, apparently insignificant ones—every moment is precious; every one is God's gift to you, and you must learn to live in it. This moment is all you have. Yesterday is gone, and nothing in the world can bring it back. You don't have that. Tomorrow is not yet, and it may never come. You have this moment.

Too many of us suffer from "someday syndrome." We put things off. We procrastinate. Procrastination is the failure to do what needs to be done when it needs to be done. So, you can procrastinate even if you're a busy person. You know you should do it, you plan on doing it, you want to do it—you just don't actually do it.

The biggest problem with this procrastination, this "someday syndrome," is that it robs you of living right now. You spend your whole life obsessing about what you should have done or what you ought to do in the future. You don't hear God's voice in this moment; you don't feel God's touch in this moment. You don't see God's grace in this moment, and the great danger is that you will never become what God intends you to be. Procrastinating is ultimately a sneaky, subtle way of saying "no" to God's call on your life.

You can learn to receive moments as gifts from God and live in them, but you will have to make a decision. It's not going to come from someplace else. The "motivation fairy" is not going to come and sprinkle motivation on you and suddenly you discover that you have learned to live in the now. You will really have to be quite serious about change.

To learn to live in the now you must:

1. Stop Excusing Procrastination.

Cut yourself off now from all the rationalizations and excuses that prop up your living for someday. You must say, "I'm going to take responsibility now for my time, my action, my life. I will own it. It's not up to somebody else. This is between God and me, and I'll need his help. The ball is in my court."

2. Take Action.

Pick one task you've been putting off. Divide it up into small steps—don't do the whole thing—and do the first step today, before you go to bed tonight. Here's what you'll discover: Motivation follows action. If you wait to do something until you feel like it or are motivated to do it, you might wait a long time. But if you take an action step even before you feel like it, you'll discover that you begin to get energized.

3. Ruthlessly Prioritize Your Life.

You've got to decide what matters and what doesn't. This is a choice of the heart. Live so that your life reflects your values—so that if somebody just looks at the way you live, they will be able to discern what matters to you or not.

4. Understand That Life, Your Life, Is Very Short.

You were made to live forever. You will be eternally alive. But your life on this earth is very short.

This is your day.
This is your moment.
This is your time. So ask
God to teach you how
to prioritize your days,
your time.
Don't let a single one
of them slip away,
not a single one.

Teach us to number our days aright,
that we may gain a heart of wisdom.

Be
Content

I have learned to be content
whatever the circumstances.

Philippians 4:11

Many people seek contentment, but it is so difficult to find. It is an elusive kind of thing. But we are called to contentment.

Conventional wisdom about contentment is that it is a result of satisfying your desires. So you think if you just had adequate financial resources or the right possessions, or the job that would really satisfy you, then you'd be content. That doesn't work, my friend.

True contentment is this—not being driven by wanting more. It is the experience of inner freedom, especially freedom from dissatisfaction, from out-of-balance appetites, from unfulfilled desires. It is freedom from that itch that says, "I've got to have it. I cannot live until I get what I don't have right now."

It is the ability to live fully in the moment. I don't have to put my life on hold until I get something or someone. Contentment is closely related to simplicity, to a simple and focused life.

Contentment is a learned skill. It is an inner ability acquired over time through practice, much in the same way as people develop the ability to make jump shots or play the piano. It is not a result of circumstances; it is the result of a certain way of living.

To know contentment you must learn how to do three things:

1. Relentlessly Establish Realistic Expectations.
Most of the time, our expectations are unrealistically high. You have to set them back down in the ballpark of reality. Contentment equals reality minus expectations.

2. Practice Gratitude for Less-Than-Perfect Gifts.

Cultivate gratitude for what you have, even for things that aren't perfect. Learn to practice thankfulness in small things, simple things, imperfect things.

3. Stake Your Life on That Which Can Satisfy Your Soul.

Contentment is not the kind of thing that can be acquired directly; it is the by-product of a certain kind of living. The apostle Paul knew this. The aim of his life was not a lifestyle of comfort and convenience; the aim of his life was to know God, to know God's kind of life, and to become God's kind of person. That is what will satisfy the human soul.

What human beings ultimately crave is the eternal. What you crave cannot be satisfied by any human circumstance or relationship or job or possession or title. It can't, because you are an eternal being, created to live for all time and beyond with God. You were created to know love and joy, and no smaller, less significant prize on earth will do it for you.

Better a little with the fear of the Lord
than great wealth with turmoil.

Proverbs 15:16

**I am always content
with what happens,
for I know that what
God chooses is better
than what I choose.**

Epictetus

Love Your

Enemies

Jesus said, "Love your enemies."

Matthew 5:44

Now the word "enemies" sounds like kind of an extreme term, and some of you may be thinking, *I don't have any enemies.* But you do, because an enemy is anybody you find hard to love. Sometimes it's the person sitting next to you. Jesus said to love them, your enemies. Do you do that? It's very hard to trust Jesus with this command of his. Something inside us says, *This is not natural! They don't deserve it. If I love them, how do I know they're going to get what's coming to them?*

Maybe your enemy is someone who has done something really bad. Maybe they've lied about you, cheated you, betrayed you, abused you, smeared your reputation, taken money from you, squelched you, or belittled you. Jesus says to love them. Jesus loved the people who killed him. He knows about enemies.

Live in
God's Peace

Let the peace of Christ rule in your hearts, to
which indeed you were called in the one body.

Colossians 3:15 (NRSV)

Learn to allow the peace of Christ to reign and rule
in your heart. God calls us very clearly to let the
peace of Christ rule in our hearts, to become a peace-
filled person. According to Dallas Willard, "The peace
of Christ is the settled assurance that because of God's
care and God's competence, this universe is a perfectly
safe place for me to be."

Paul said, "What can separate us from the love of
God?" Then he listed all kinds of terrible things in this
world that seem to be peace-shattering: danger, famine,
sword, persecution, death itself. All of these things
threaten to shatter our peace. But Paul said that nothing
can separate us from the love of God. And when you
live in that subtle assurance, it changes your life.

Jesus said, "In this world you will have trouble.
But take heart! I have overcome the world."

John 16:33

The mind of sinful man is death, but the
mind controlled by the Spirit is life and peace.

Romans 8:6

Let us therefore make every effort to do what
leads to peace and to mutual edification.

Romans 14:19

A converted Hindu who had been given a Bible and a clock said, "The clock will tell me how time goes, and the Bible will tell me how to spend it."

Anonymous

Use Your Time
Well

Remember your Creator
in the days of your youth,
before the days of trouble come
and the years approach when you will say,
"I find no pleasure in them."

Ecclesiastes 12:1

Make the best use of your time. Don't be vague, but grasp firmly what you know to be the will of God.

Have you ever done anything that made you feel stupid? Well, I did. Here it is. One year my family spent the week between Christmas and New Year's Day with relatives. The night we flew home to Chicago, we got a ride from O'Hare back to our house with a driver we didn't know. It was bitter cold and snowy and way past midnight. On the way home in the van, Nancy turned to me and said, "Do you have any way to get back in the house when we get home?" I said, "No.

It never occurred to me. Don't you have a key?"

It seemed kind of a wife's thing to me to think about the keys. She replied, "No, it never occurred to me, either."

There we were. It was late, it was freezing cold, and the kids didn't even have coats on because we had been where it was warm, and we were locked out of our own house! I had to break a window to get into my house that night. What a stupid thing to have to do!

But every day there are people who do something infinitely dumber than not being able to get into their own house. They can't get into their own lives. They're trapped, running some idiot race on a tread-mill that's never going to stop.

I can't imagine this for me. I can't imagine this for you: standing before God one day and having God say, "I made you; I created you; I thought you out before the advent of the world. I sent my Son to die on a cross to redeem you. I made you think great, wonderful, deep thoughts, to pray tremendous prayers, to offer great life-giving worship, to raise great families, to be a gift to those who are poor, to be a light to people who were lost and needed to be brought home. I made you for that. Why didn't you do it?"

I can't imagine standing there on that day and saying to God, "I was too busy." In God's name, too busy doing what?

Whatever you do, do whatever you need to do to lead a sane, joy-giving, God-honoring, love-producing way of life. And then someday, maybe tomorrow, maybe many, many years from now, you can stand together with God, look back on your life, and say, "I didn't do it perfectly, but I did the best I could. God, with the help of your Spirit, I chose the great adventure of growing up into Christ."

It's your call.

Live life, then, with a due sense of responsibility, not as men who do not know the meaning and purpose of life but as those who do.

Ephesians 5:15 (PHILLIPS)

Sources:

Buechner, Frederick. *Beyond Words: Daily Reading in the ABC's of Faith.* © 2004 by Frederick Buechner. San Francisco: HarperCollins, 2004.

De Pree, Max. *Leadership Is An Art.* © 1989 by Max De Pree. New York: Doubleday, 1989.

de Vinck, Christopher. *Simple Wonders: The Disarming Pleasure of Looking Beyond the Seen.* © 1995 by Christopher de Vinck. Grand Rapids, MI: ZondervanPublishingHouse, 1995.

Lamott, Anne. *Traveling Mercies: Some Thoughts on Faith.* © 1999 by Anne Lamott. New York: Anchor Books, 1999.

Luther, Martin. *By Faith Alone.* © 1998 by World Publishing. Grand Rapids, MI: World Publishing, 1998.

Men's Devotional Bible, New International Version. © 1993 by the Zondervan Corporation. Grand Rapids, MI: ZondervanPublishingHouse, 1993.

Walsh, Sheila. *Gifts for Your Soul.* © 1997 by Sheila Walsh. Grand Rapids, MI: ZondervanPublishingHouse, 1997.

Wilson Schaef, Anne. *Meditations for Women Who Do Too Much.* © 1990 by Anne Wilson Schaef. San Francisco: Harper & Row, 1990.

At Inspirio, we love to hear from you—
your stories, your feedback,
and your product ideas.
Please send your comments to us
by way of e-mail at
icares@zondervan.com
or to the address below:

ᵞ
inspirio™

Attn: Inspirio Cares
5300 Patterson Avenue SE
Grand Rapids, MI 49530

If you would like further information
about Inspirio and the products we
create please visit us at:
www.inspiriogifts.com

Thank you and God bless!